Before Using...

 Before using this book, please read the guidelines inside the back cover. For a free copy of the detailed guidelines go to www.hunterhouse.com or call the ordering number below.

 To prevent bleed-through, it is recommended that water-based, rather than spirit-based, markers or pens be used in this Workbook.

Someone I Love Died

A Hunter House Growth and Recovery Workbook
by Wendy Deaton, M.A., M.F.C.C.
Series consultant: Kendall Johnson, Ph.D.

ISBN-13: 978-1-63026-831-2

Ordering Information

Additional copies of this and other Growth and Recovery Workbooks may be obtained from Hunter House. Bulk discounts are available for professional offices and recognized organizations.

All single workbooks: $11.95

The Growth and Recovery Workbooks (GROW) Series

A creative, child-friendly program designed for use with elementary-school children, filled with original exercises to foster healing, self-understanding, and optimal growth.

Workbooks for children ages 9–12 include:

No More Hurt—provides a safe place for children who have been physically or sexually abused to explore and share their feelings

Living with My Family—helps children traumatized by domestic violence and family fights to identify and express their fears

Someone I Love Died—for children who have lost a loved one and who are dealing with grief, loss, and helplessness

A Separation in My Family—for children whose parents are separating or have already separated or divorced

Drinking and Drugs in My Family—for children who have family members who engage in regular alcohol and substance abuse

I Am a Survivor—for children who have survived an accident or fire, or a natural disaster such as a flood, hurricane, or earthquake

I Saw It Happen—for children who have witnessed a traumatic event such as a shooting at school, a frightening accident, or other violence

Workbooks for children ages 6–10 include:

My Own Thoughts and Feelings (for Girls); My Own Thoughts and Feelings (for Boys)—for exploring suspected trauma and early symptoms of depression, low self-esteem, family conflict, maladjustment, and nonspecific dysfunction

My Own Thoughts on Stopping the Hurt—for exploring suspected trauma and communicating with young children who may have suffered physical or sexual abuse

We welcome suggestions for new and needed workbooks

You are SPECIAL.
Write your name
here in a
special way.

This is your book.
In it you can write about
yourself and your feelings.

Draw a picture
of how you feel
today.

2

Make a list of special things about you.

_____

_____

_____

_____

_____

_____

_____

_____

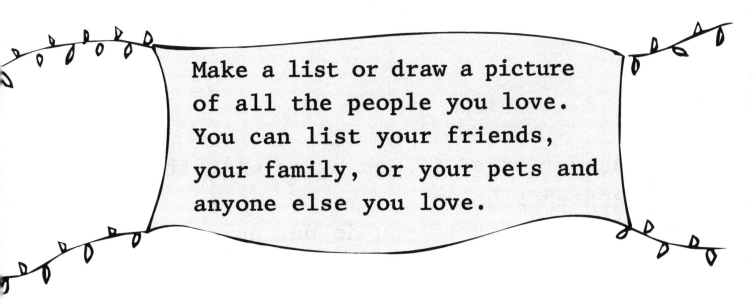

Make a list or draw a picture of all the people you love. You can list your friends, your family, or your pets and anyone else you love.

Answer "Yes" if you agree with the sentence below.
Answer "No" if you do not agree.

❀ Love makes you happy._____

❀ Love sometimes hurts._____

❀ There are a many of kinds of love._____

❀ Love lasts forever._____

❀ Loving always feels good._____

❀ Love means you are always together._____

❀ Love never dies._____

Sometimes love hurts. It hurts when someone you love goes away. It hurts a lot when someone you love dies. Draw a picture of how love hurts.

6

Draw a picture of the
person you love who died.

What do you think happens when
you die?
Draw a picture or write about
what you think happens.

_____

_____

_____

_____

_____

_____

_____

_____

_____

_____

_____

People die for a lot of
different reasons. Make a list
of reasons why people die.

9

Write about why you think
the person you love died.

_____

_____

_____

_____

_____

_____

_____

_____

_____

_____

_____

_____

Draw a picture of how it
feels when you think about
the person who died.

Who told you about the dying?
Draw a picture of you finding
out about what happened.

write about how it felt
when you found out what
happened.

When someone you love dies, you have a lot of different feelings. Here are some feelings people have when they lose someone they love:

☐ sad   ☐ guilty   ☐ like screaming

☐ angry   ☐ scared   ☐ like hitting

☐ mixed up   ☐ worried   ☐ sorry

☐ mad   ☐ lonely

☐ glad they didn't hurt any more

Check all the feelings
        you have.

Any others:

_____

_____

_____

14

Here are some things you might
be scared or worried about:

     ⁕ scared you might die too

     ⁕ scared someone else you love might die

     ⁕ worried how it feels to be dead

     ⁕ worried about the person who died

     ⁕ scared it was your fault they died

Write about anything that worries
or scares you.

_____

_____

_____

_____

_____

_____

_____

Here are some things that might make you angry:

❀ angry because someone you love left you

❀ angry because it hurts to miss someone

❀ angry because it hurts to be scared

❀ angry because everyone around you is sad

❀ angry because you can't do things now that you want to do

❀ angry because you feel like you can't have fun now

❀ angry at God for taking someone you love away

❀ angry at the doctors for not helping more

©1994 Wendy Deaton and Hunter House Inc.

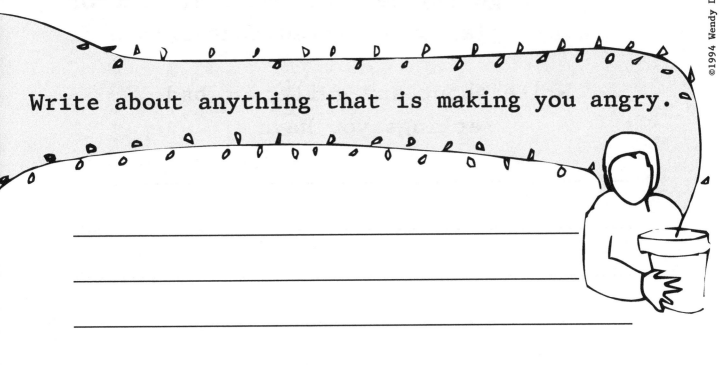

Write about anything that is making you angry.

_____

_____

_____

_____

_____

Here are some things that might make you feel guilty or bad:

❦ guilty because you were angry or had a fight just before the person died

❦ guilty because you don't feel sad or because you can't cry

❦ guilty because you think it is your fault the person died

❦ guilty because you feel kind of glad or relieved that it's over

Write about any guilty or bad feelings you have.

_____

_____

_____

_____

_____

_____

Here are some reasons you might feel glad:

❦ glad because the person isn't hurting anymore

❦ glad because the person isn't sick anymore

❦ glad because the person is at peace now

❦ glad because you can pay attention to other things

Write about any glad feelings you have.

_____

_____

_____

_____

_____

_____

_____

_____

Whatever feelings you have are okay. Feelings are not right or wrong, good or bad, they are just feelings.

You do not have control over what you feel, your feelings just happen to you. You can only control what you do about your feelings.

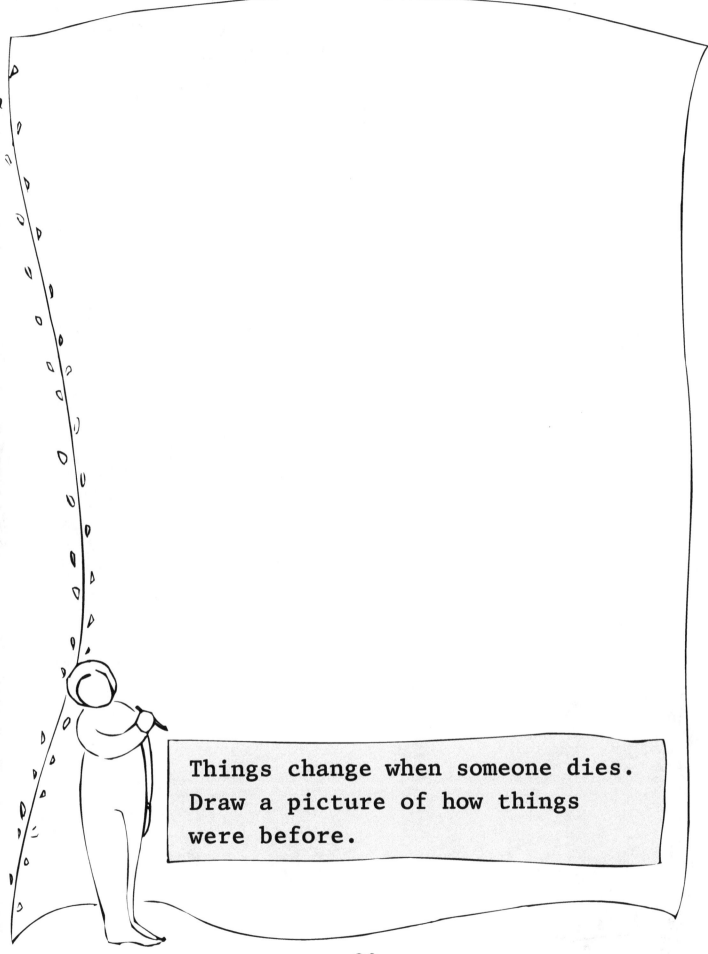

Things change when someone dies. Draw a picture of how things were before.

Draw a picture of
how things are
different now.

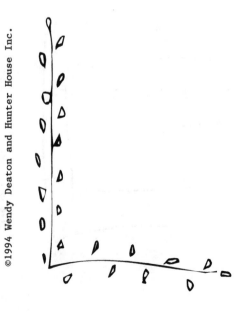

21

When someone you love dies, you miss them. You miss doing things together and special things you shared.

Make a list of the things that you miss now.

Are there things you would like to say to the person who died? Write a letter telling them what you would say if you could talk to them right now.

Has anyone else you loved died or gone away? Or have you ever been very sad about something? Draw a picture to show what happened or how you felt then.

24

_____

_____

_____

_____

_____

_____

_____

_____

_____

_____

If you have ever lost someone else, or if you have ever been very sad about something that happened to you, write about what helped to make you feel better that time.

When someone you love dies, you may feel lonely.

What are some things you can do to make yourself feel better when you are lonely?

_____

_____

_____

_____

_____

_____

_____

_____

_____

_____

Make a list of all the people you can talk to who can help you feel better about someone you love dying.

Here are some problems you might have in your life. Next to the problem put the name of the person who can help you with the problem:

❦ help you with homework _____

❦ help when you are sick _____

❦ help with problems with friends _____

❦ help you have fun _____

❦ help with sad feelings _____

❦ help with angry feelings _____

❦ help with other feelings _____

❦ help when you feel lonely _____

Write about or draw a picture of something good that has happened to you since the person you loved died.

Write or draw a picture
about your favorite memory
of the person who died.

If you could make three wishes,
what would your wishes be?

_____

_____

_____

_____

_____

_____

_____

_____

_____

_____

_____

_____

_____

Write a story about the future with a happy ending.

32

PLEASE READ THIS...

This is a brief guide to the design and use of the Growth and Recovery (GROW) workbooks from Hunter House. It is excerpted from detailed guidelines that can be downloaded from www.hunterhouse.com or are available free through the mail by calling the ordering number at the bottom of the page. Please consult the detailed guidelines before using this workbook for the first time.

GROW workbooks provide a way to open up communication with children who are not able to or who are reluctant to talk about a traumatic experience. They are not self-help books and are not designed for guardians or parents to use on their own with children. They address sensitive issues, and a child's recovery and healing require the safety, structured approach, and insight provided by a trained professional.

Each therapist will bring her own originality, creativity, and experience to the interaction and may adapt the tasks and activities in the workbooks, using other materials and activities. With less verbally oriented children, the use of art therapy or music or video may be recommended, or certain exercises may be conducted in groups.

Each pair of facing pages in the workbook provides the focus for a therapeutic "movement" that may take up one session. However, more than one movement can be made in a single session or several sessions may be devoted to a single movement. Children should be allowed to move through the process at their own pace. If a child finds a task too "hot" to approach, the therapist can return to it later. When something is fruitful it can be pursued with extended tasks.

While a therapist is free to select the order of activities for each child, the exercises are laid out in a progression based on the principles of critical incident stress management:

- initial exercises focus on building the therapeutic alliance
- the child is then led to relate an overview of the experience
- this is deepened by a "sensory-unpacking" designed to access and recover traumatic memories
- family experiences and changed living conditions, if any, are explored
- emotions are encouraged, explored, and validated.
- delayed reactions are dealt with, and resources are explored.
- the experience is integrated into the child's life through a series of strength-building exercises.

Specific pages in the GROW workbooks are cross-referenced to Dr. Kendall Johnson's book *Trauma in the Lives of Children* (Hunter House, Alameda, 1998). This provides additional information on the treatment of traumatized children.

The content of the workbooks should be shared with parents or significant adults only when the child feels ready for it and if it is therapeutically wise. Workbooks should not be given to children to take home until the therapeutic process is completed according to the therapist's satisfaction.

Although this series of workbooks was written for school-age children, the tasks are adaptable for use with younger children and adolescents.

Detailed guidelines are available for each GROW workbook (see list on front inside cover).

CPSIA information can be obtained
at www.ICGtesting.com
Printed in the USA
LVHW101649030720
659689LV00018B/323